Sunshine

Pupil's Book

Class 4

EARLY START EDITION

Cornelsen

Sunshine **Early Start Edition**
Lehrwerk für den früh beginnenden Englischunterricht

Pupil's Book 4
Class 4

Erarbeitet von
Birgit Hollbrügge, Bielefeld; Ulrike Kraaz, Werther

unter Mitarbeit von
Dagmar Lehmann, Tangermünde; Ines Völtz, Leipzig

Beratende Mitwirkung
Katja Bosse, Braunschweig; Uwe Becker, Mannheim; Karin Freund, Triebes; Evelin Hartmann-Kleinschmidt, Delbrück; Ingrid-Barbara Hoffmann, Böblingen; Karin Kania, Berlin; Inge Kronisch, Flensburg; Dagmar Lehmann, Tangermünde; Petra Ilona Sälzer, Kamen; Christel Simon, Spreenhagen; Silke Thiel, Erzhausen; Ines Völtz, Leipzig
sowie Kathrin Barnath, Königswalde; Myriam Czepluch, Sinzig; Margarete Frederichs, Paderborn; Ute Gebhardt, Blankenburg; Miriam Habermann, Ratingen; Renate Hafner, Blaustein; Fred Hamann, Gera; Helen Paul, Leussow; Susanne Putler, Langenzenn; Dietlinde Rack, Friedberg; Katja Todtenhaupt-Duscha, Braunschweig; Vera Windmüller, Paderborn

Verlagsredaktion
Marie Keenoy (Projektleitung), Annette Burs, Elke Lehmann, Penny Paulus, Stefanie Schindewolf

Illustration
Beehive Illustration, Cirencester, England: Neil Chapman, Mike Phillips; Mary Hall, Bath, England

Umschlaggestaltung
Karla Detlefsen, Berlin

Layout
Susanne Meyer

Technische Umsetzung
Jana Faust, Berlin; Susanne Meyer

Quellenangaben
Bildquellen Alamy, Abingdon (S. 5 Big Ben: Matthew Lodge; S. 6 London Eye: Ian Macpherson, Big Ben: JUPITERIMAGES/ Polka Dot; S. 8 Madame Tussauds: Jon Arnold Images Ltd; S. 10 Ankara: Ken Welsh, Rom: Scott Hortop, London: John Norman; S.13 Sturm: Stockbyte; S. 25 Central Park: David Ball, Taxis: Steve Hamblin, Dollar: kolvenback; S. 28 Little Italy: Robert Fried, Chinatown: Alan Schein; S. 37 Mädchen: Ilene MacDonald); Avenue Images, Hamburg (S. 10 New York: image 100, S. 35 Santa Claus: stockdisc); Francis Cony, Bristol (S. 36 Valentinskarte); Getty images, München (S. 8 Wachsfigur: Sion Touhig, Figuren aus Wachs: Madonna: Lio Song; Justin Timberlake: Anthony Harvey, Johnny Depp: Barry King, David Beckham: Tim Whitby, Queen Elizabeth: Barry King; S. 28 Dirk Nowitzki: Tim Heitman); Irish Image Collection (S. 37 Parade, Irish Dancing); Rebecca Kaplan, Berlin (S. 5 Buckingham Palace, S. 14 Löwe, Dinosaurier, Krokodil); Ulrike Kraaz & Birgit Hollbrügge (S. 11); Mexx, Hamburg (S. 33 Kleid); National History Museum, London (S. 14 Elefant, Papagei, Wal, Museum); Michael Pead, Birningham (S. 5 London Zoo); Photolibary: S. 28 Mexican food: Roy Morsch; Royal Mail (S. 6 Briefmarken); Marion Schönenberger, Berlin (S. 8, 13, 18, 23, 28 Anweisungen); Shutterstock (S. 5 Tower Bridge: Jarno Gonzalez Zarraonadia, London Eye: Bryan Busovicki, River Thames: David Burrows; S. 6 Tower Bridge: WizData, inc; S. 10 Miami: Jonathan Larsen, Paris: rfx; S. 13 Wäsche: Peter Elvidge, Tornado: Matsonashvili Mikhail, Windrad: James Thew, Auto: Graham Prentice, Segelboot: Greg Kushmerek; S. 17: Afrikanischer Elefant: Jonathan Heger, Indischer Elefant: Micha Fleuren; S. 23 Mädchen auf Fahrrad: Olga Vasilkova, Mädchen am Fußballspielen: Rob Marmion; Jungen: Sonya Etchison; S. 25 Wolkenkratzer: Zina Seletsays, Empire State Building: Ian Klein, Statue of Liberty: Rajesh Pattabiraman; Cent: Yegor Korzh; Brooklyn Bridge: Johnny Kuo; S. 28 Parade: Michael Rubin, S. 33 Elefant: David Hamman; Papagei: Xavier Marchant, Löwe: Keith Levit, Wal: Jan Daly; S. 35 Mistelzweig: Lisa F. Young, Strumpf: Michele Bagdon; Zuckerstangen: Edyta Pawlowska; S. 37, Kleeblatt: 8781118005); Stills Online, Hamburg (S. 33 Schuhe, Hose); theofeel Kindermode, Dresden (S. 33 Mütze)
Textquelle: S. 36 „Issue Year" by Highlights for Children, Inc., Columbus, Ohio.

Weitere Bestandteile des Lehrwerkes *Sunshine Early Start Edition*:

Activity Book mit Audio-CD Kurzfassung	ISBN 978-3-464-34693-8
Activity Book mit Audio-CD Kurzfassung und kompletter Lernsoftware	ISBN 978-3-06-031293-1
Lernsoftware	ISBN 978-3-06-031435-5

www.cornelsen.de

1. Auflage, 1. Druck 2009

Druck: CS-Druck CornelsenStürtz, Berlin

ISBN 978-3-464-34696-9

Inhalt gedruckt auf säurefreiem Papier aus nachhaltiger Forstwirtschaft.

Contents

Symbols

CD 1.8 listen to the CD · CD 1 track 8

listen

speak

read

play

Back at school

1 Look at the picture. Talk about the picture.

2 Read the speech bubbles with a partner.

3 Talk about holidays. Ask a partner three questions.

What's in the classroom?

Write a list.

There's …

There are …

1 A trip to London

London sights

CD 1.9

1 Listen. Where do Harry, Kate and Kate's dad go?

3

2

1

6

4

5

Dialogue: Buying tickets

1 Read the dialogue.

2 Talk to a partner.

Postcards from London

1 Look at the pictures. Talk about the pictures.

2 Read the postcards. Say the numbers.

3 When was Harry's birthday?
What's the name of Harry's grandma?

1

2

3

Dear Mum,

I like London. It's great! This is Tower Bridge. What a big bridge! You must go and see Tower Bridge. See you on Saturday.

Love, Kate

Mrs
12 M
Band

Dear Grandma,

It's Tuesday. I'm in London. London is great. Here's Big Ben. What a big clock tower!

Love, Harry

Mrs Benson,
5 Birch Street,
Portsmouth,
Hants PO12 2TB

...ck Stuart

Hello Jack,

I'm in London with Kate. It's super! Thursday was my birthday. I was on the London Eye. It was great.

Harry

Texte lesen und zuordnen (S. 81)

Story: A whale in the River Thames

1 Look at the pictures. Talk about the pictures.

CD 1.11 **2 Listen. Point to the right pictures.**

3 Read the story. Act it out.

1

There was a whale in the River Thames.

On Thursday the whale was under Tower Bridge.
'Wow, what a big bridge!'

2

On Friday there was the London Eye.
'Wow, what a big wheel!'

3

On Saturday there was Big Ben.
'Wow, what a big clock tower!'

But the whale wasn't happy.
'Where's my mum? Where's my dad?'

4

5

'Bye-bye, Big Ben.'
'Bye-bye, London Eye.'
'Bye-bye, Tower Bridge.'

6

On Sunday he said:
'Hello, Mum. Hello, Dad.'

Spotlight: A London museum

1 Read the text about the museum.

Madame Tussauds is a museum in London.

There are famous people in the museum: pop stars, film stars, sport stars and kings and queens.

The people in the museum are made of wax.

2 Look at the pictures. Talk to a partner about the people.

Madonna
David Beckham
Johnny Depp
Queen Elizabeth II
Justin Timberlake

3 Make your own museum.

You need:

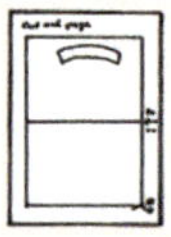
cut-out page

pictures

scissors

glue

coloured pencils

1 Cut out the card.
Write the name of your museum on the card.

2 Fold the card in the middle.
Cut along the dotted lines.

3 Open the card.
Pull out the strips.

4 Glue the pictures on the strips.

Here's my museum.

Texte lesen, Informationen entnehmen, eine Bastelanleitung befolgen (S.191)

A rainy day

1 Look at all the pictures. Talk about the pictures.

2 Read the speech bubbles.

3 What's the weather like in the pictures?

4 What are the children doing? Say the sentences.

Emily
Harry
Harry and Emily
Kate
Samir
The children

are playing hopscotch · are waiting for the bus
is eating an ice cream · is in London
is making a snowman · is walking in the park with his dog

Dialogue: What's the weather like?

1 Read the dialogue.

2 Talk to a partner.

Ankara

Paris

New York

Rome

London

Miami

Einen Dialog sprechen (S.95)

My birthday

1 **Read the texts.** 2 **Talk about the pictures.**

The boys are drawing pictures.

2 All year round

Portfolio:
My birthday month

1 **Write the month. Number the days in your calendar.**

September

MON	TUE	WED	THU	FRI	SAT	SUN
1	2	3	4	5	6	7
8	9	10	11	12	13	14
15	16	17	18	19	20	21
22	23	24	25	26	27	28
29	30					

2 **Complete the sentences.**

My name is Mia

My birthday is in September.

September is in autumn.

The weather in September :

It's sunny and cloudy. It's windy.

3 **Draw or glue things from your birthday month.**

16 sixteen Über Monate, Wochentage und das Wetter sprechen (S. 100)

The girl is presenting her page.

Board game: The four seasons

1 Read the sentences.

2 Play the game.

START	1 Go forward 2.	2 It's a snowy Saturday in January.	3	4	5 Snowdrops in winter.	6
7 A birthday in March.	8	9 Daffodils in spring.	10	11 It's 25° on Sunday.	12 It's a rainy Monday in June.	13 Go back 3.
14 It's a cold Tuesday in summer.	15	16 Throw again.	17 Red roses in July.	18	19 We have summer holidays.	20 It's a sunny Wednesday in August.
21	22 It's a cloudy Friday in September.	23 It's a windy Thursday in October.	24 Spiders in autumn.	25	26 Miss a turn.	27 It's a foggy Monday in November.
28	29 It's 15° on Christmas Day.	30	FINISH			

Einen Spielplan lesen · ein Brettspiel spielen (S.101, 102)

Spotlight: The wind

1 When is the wind helpful? When is the wind dangerous?
Talk about the pictures. Say: In picture 1, the wind is …

1

2

3

4

5

6

2 Read the rhyme.

The kites go up, the kites go down.
See how they fly all over the town.
The children run and jump and play,
Because they love a windy day.

3 Do the experiment with your teacher.

You need:

a bottle

a candle

matches

1 Put the candle behind the bottle.

2 Blow hard on the bottle.
What happens to the candle?

Animals in the museum

1 **What animals are in the museum?**

2 **Read the speech bubbles.**

3 **Talk to a partner.**

What other animals do you know?
Write a list.

OPEN
Monday–Sunday
10.00–17.50

Sätze lesen, Aussagen zu Abbildungen machen (S.107)

Dialogue: Where are the animals?

1 Read the dialogue.

2 Talk to a partner.

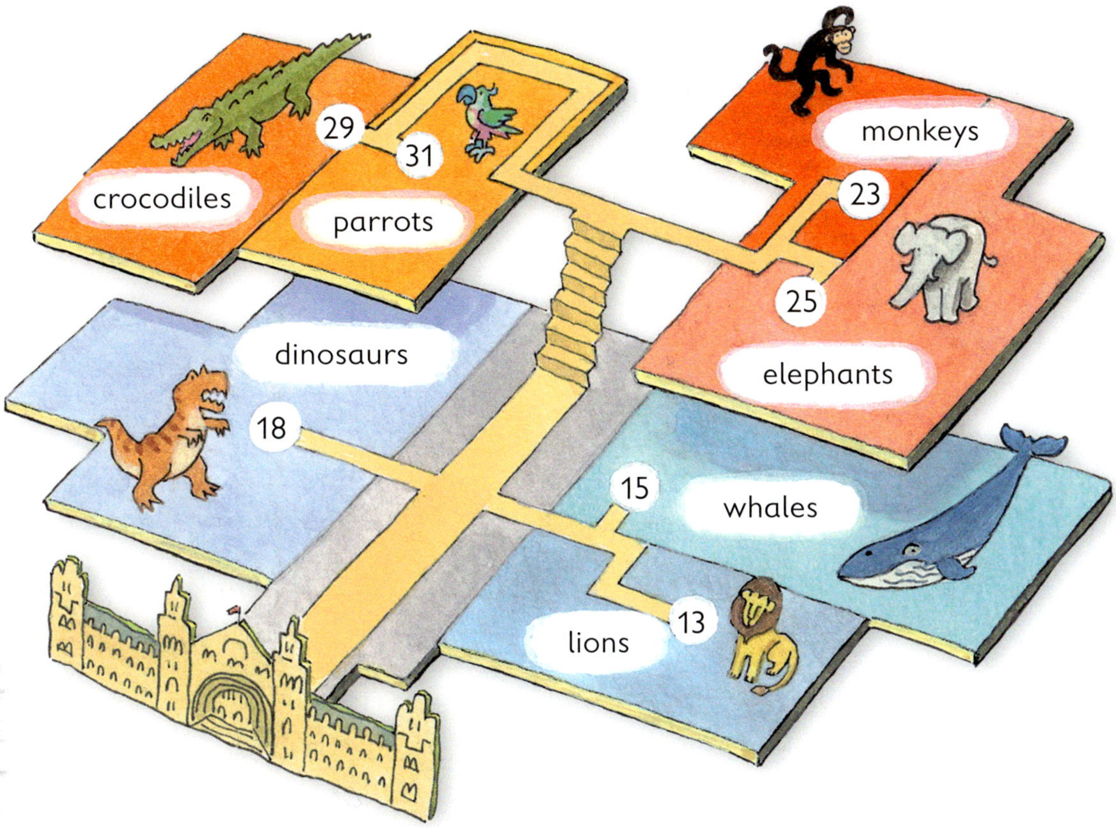

About wild animals

1 Read the texts.

2 Talk about the mole.

3 Read the rules for your presentation.

Make notes.

Know your text.

Speak loudly.

Look at the class.

Show pictures.

 Texte lesen/Tiere beschreiben (S. 116) · besprechen, wie man einen Vortrag hält (S. 117)

Story: Harry's night at the museum

1 **Look at the pictures. Talk about the pictures.**

2 **Read the speech bubbles.**

Spotlight: Elephants

1 Read the texts.

This elephant lives in Africa. It lives in the savannah. It eats grass. It has got big ears. The teeth of an elephant are long and white. They're called tusks.

This elephant lives in India. It lives in the forest. It eats leaves. It has got small ears. The nose of an elephant is called a trunk.

2 Make an elephant mask.

You need:

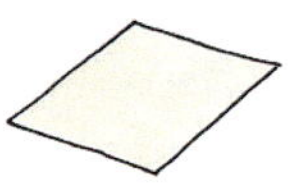
cardboard

a pencil

scissors

a stapler

glue

string

1 Draw the ears, trunk and tusks on the cardboard. Cut them out.

2 Place the ears on the face. Staple the ears to the face.

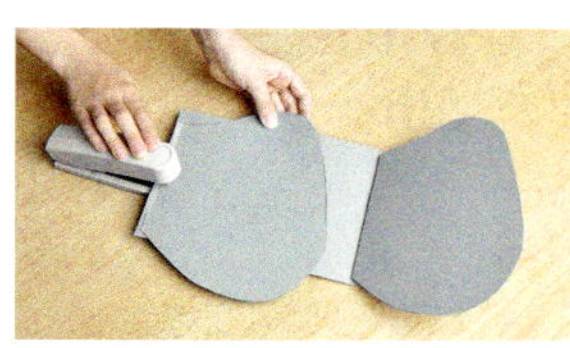

3 Cut out the eyes and make holes for the string.

4 Glue on the trunk.

5 Glue on the tusks.

Here's your elephant mask.

Sachtexte lesen, eine Tiermaske basteln (S.195)

4 Keeping fit

School clubs

1 **Read the texts. What clubs are there?**

2 **Work with a partner. Talk about the clubs.**

3 **Listen. Which club do the children want to go to?**

CD 1.28

Where's the dance club?

It's in …

When's the computer club?

It's on …

Rhyme: Animal moves

CD 1.29

1 Listen to the rhyme. Point to the pictures.

2 Read the rhyme.

3

2

4

Can you walk like a cat?
Can you eat like a rat?
Can you sit like a dog?
Can you hop like a frog?
Can you run like a horse?
Yes, I can, of course.

1

5

Fitness in the classroom

1 Work with a partner. Say the action.

What can Kate do?

1 **Which activities are there?**

2 **Say what Kate can and can't do.**

3 **Listen. Were you right?**

CD 1.31

1

2

3

7

4

6

5

Dialogue: Sport

1 **Read the dialogue.**

dance · play basketball
play football · ski · swim

2 **Talk to a partner about other sports.**

Story: Emily the sports star

1 **Talk about the pictures.**

2 **Listen to the story.**

CD 1.32

3 **Read the story.**

Eine Geschichte verstehen und lesen (S.137)

Spotlight: My body

… is good for my body.

… isn't good for my body.

1 Read the sentences. Say what's good for your body.

1 I like swimming in the summer.
2 I often go cycling with my friends.
3 I love football.
4 I like playing computer games and watching TV.
5 Running is my favourite sport.
6 My favourite food is chocolate.
7 I do yoga every Monday.

2 What else is good for your body? Talk to a partner.

3 Read the words and find the right pictures.

That's yoga:
1 The Tree
2 The Plane
3 The Crocodile

4 Check your pulse.

1 Put two fingers on your wrist. Count your pulse for 15 seconds.

2 Hop on one leg through the classroom for 2 minutes.

3 Count your pulse again for 15 seconds. Is it the same?

5 Emails from the USA

E-pals

1 Talk about the picture.

2 Read the questions.

3 Answer the questions.

What's your name?	*Kate*
How old are you?	*I'm 10 years old.*
When's your birthday?	*May* *26*
Where are you from?	*I'm from Great Britain.*
What's your nickname?	*Kitty*
What's your password?	*Supergirl*
What are your hobbies?	*dancing, swimming*

Ein Formular lesen, Fragen zur Person beantworten (S. 143)

New York

1 Read the sentences. Match the pictures.

This is the Statue of Liberty.

The Empire State Building is the biggest skyscraper in New York.

There are a lot of skyscrapers in New York.

Americans use dollars and cents to buy things.

You can see many yellow taxis in New York.

Brooklyn Bridge is a very old bridge.

Central Park is a big park in the middle of New York.

Dialogue: Where do you live?

1 Read the dialogue.

2 Talk to a partner.

Emails to Matt and Kate

1 **Read Kate's email.**

2 **What questions can Kate ask?**

About my family

To: mattman@world.e-pals.com
Subject: About my family

Dear Matt,
Today I want to write about my family. I live with my mum and dad. My dad has got a second-hand shop and my mum is a hairdresser. I've got a big sister. She's 18 and she's a shop assistant.
I haven't got a brother but I've got a lot of friends. My best friends are Harry, Samir and Emily. We like playing in Harry's garden and in the street. What do you like?
My grandmother lives in London – what a great city! I was there in September with Harry and my dad.

What about you?

What's your mum's and your dad's job?

Work with a dictionary.

CD 2.5 **3** **Listen to Matt's email.**

4 **Read the text.**

About me

To: kitty@world.e-pals.com
Subject: About me

Hi Kate,
Thanks for your email. I'm ten years old. My birthday is in November.
I've got a brother. He's a mechanic. And I've got a baby sister. My mother is a teacher. My father works in the city. He's a taxi driver. I've got two hamsters. I like playing with my hamsters. My hobbies are playing computer games and reading. What are your hobbies?

Your friend,
Matt

Texte lesen und verstehen (S. 149, 151)

Story: A day in New York

1 Read the story.

Spotlight: The USA

1 Read the sentences. Match the pictures.

(1)

(2)

(3)

Some people from **Ireland** live in the USA.
In March there's a big **Irish** parade in New York.
Everybody wears green clothes.

(4)

Some people from **Germany** live in the USA.
In the picture you see a **German** basketball player.

Some people from **China** live in the USA.
There are a lot of **Chinese** shops in American cities.

Some people from **Italy** live in the USA.
This house is green, white and red.
The **Italian** flag is green, white and red, too.

(5)

Some people from **Mexico** live in the USA.
Do you like **Mexican** food?

2 Make a Mexican wrap.

You need:

a wrap

carrots

cheese

chili sauce

lettuce

sour cream

1 Put sour cream and lettuce on your wrap.

2 Grate some carrots and cheese. Put it on the wrap.

3 Put some chili sauce on the wrap.

4 Fold your wrap.

Enjoy your Mexican wrap.

Landeskundliche Informationen erfahren, ein Rezept befolgen (S.199)

Board game: Welcome to New York

1 Play the game. Your teacher gives you the sentences.

● Read the sentences. Miss a turn. ● Read the sentences. Throw again.

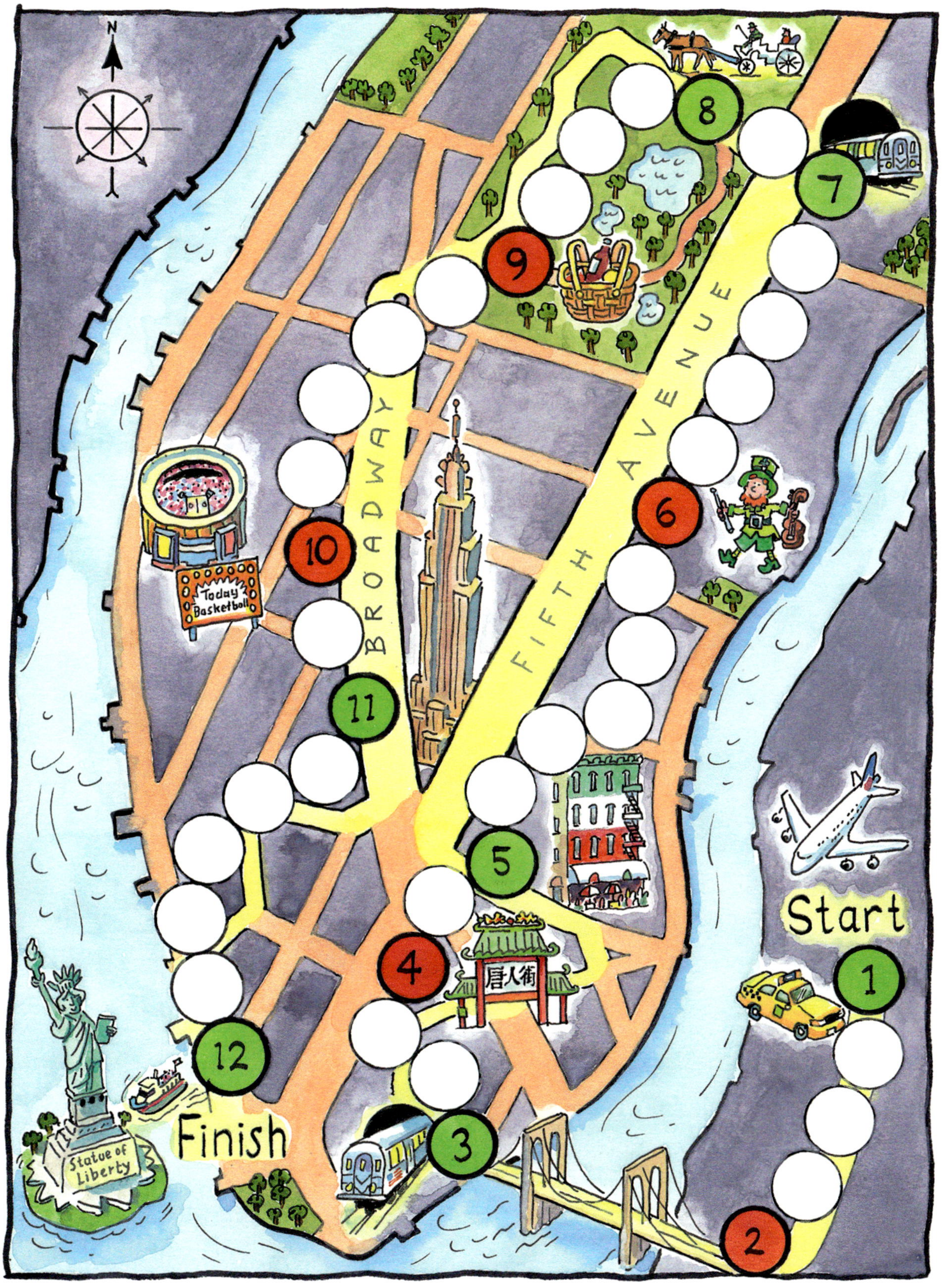

6 A school play

Story: The school inspector

1 Read the story.

Aussagen zu Abbildungen machen und Sprechblasen lesen (S. 161)

6
Do you know a rhyme?
Of course, we do!
I can say: The elephant goes like this and that.
7
I'm very angry. What a bad class.
8
Can you read?
Of course, we can!
There was a whale in the River Thames.
9
That was bad!
No, that isn't right, inspector.
10
I'm not the school inspector. Sorry, Mrs Brown.
He's the caretaker!
He isn't the school inspector.
11
Thank you, Ms Honey. They're good pupils.
What a nice class, Mrs Brown!

Do you know the rhymes?

1 **Read the rhyme and chants.**

The elephant

The elephant goes
Like this, like that.
He's terribly big,
And he's terribly fat.
He has no fingers,
He has big toes,
And goodness gracious,
What a nose!

Holidays

I was in London,
She was in Rome,
He was in Ankara,
And where were you?
I was at home.

Feed your pets

Please drink your milk and eat your bread.
Yes, Mum, yes.
Please feed your dog in the garden shed.
Yes, Dad, yes.

Please drink your tea and eat your bread.
Yes, Mum, yes.
Please feed your pets and go to bed.
Yes, Dad, yes.
Night, night.

Looking back at Sunshine

1 **Look at the pictures. Read the texts.**

2 **Did you like your English book?**

3 **What else can you remember?**

I don't like … because …

That was OK.

I know the colours.

That was great!

My favourite song was "Head, shoulders …"

I know about New York.

That wasn't so good.

Units

At school

In the park

All year round

Keeping fit

Word fields

Clothes

Wild animals

Songs

Listen to the rain

Pitter-patter. Pitter-patter.
Listen to the rain.
Pitter-patter. Pitter-patter.
On the windowpane.

Pitter-pat. Pitter-pat.
What is that? What is that?
One big raindrop on my hat.

If you're happy

If you're happy and you know it,
clap your hands.
If you're happy and you know it,
clap your hands.
If you're happy and you know it,
and you really want to show it.
If you're happy and you know it,
clap your hands.

Dialogues

7 Special days

Bonfire Night

1 Read the story of Guy Fawkes.

2 Talk about the pictures.

3 Listen. Read the rhyme.

CD 2.22

Penny for the guy!

Remember, remember
The fifth of November.
Gunpowder, treason and plot.
I see no reason
Why gunpowder treason
Should ever be forgot.

Die Geschichte von Guy Fawkes lesen, landeskundliche Informationen erfahren (S.179), einen Reim lernen (S.181)

Christmas

1 Read the rhyme.

Christmas is near

Good evening, children,
Christmas is near.
My name's Santa Claus
That's my 

Brrr, it is windy
and it is cold.
I have got 
for young and for old.

Open your eyes,
what do you see?
A big and shiny 

2 Listen to the song. Sing the song.

CD 2.24

Santa Claus is coming

Valentine's Day

1 Read the cards.

2 Which card is your favourite? Read it to a partner.

3 Read the story.

The world's smallest valentine

It was Valentine's Day.
Olivia gave her grandpa a piece of folded paper.
'It's the world's smallest valentine', she said.

Grandpa opened it.
'It's a seed,' he said.
'Why is a seed the world's smallest valentine?'
'Because it's a tomato seed,' said Olivia.
'The old name for tomato is love apple.
It's a love apple seed.'

Grandpa smiled.
'That's a wonderful valentine,' he said.

Landeskundliche Informationen erfahren · sich zu Bildern äußern, eine Geschichte lesen (S.185)

Saint Patrick's Day

1 Talk about the pictures.

The shamrock has three leaves.

This is Irish dancing.

This is a parade on Saint Patrick's Day.

Everybody wears green clothes.

2 Read Fiona's letter.

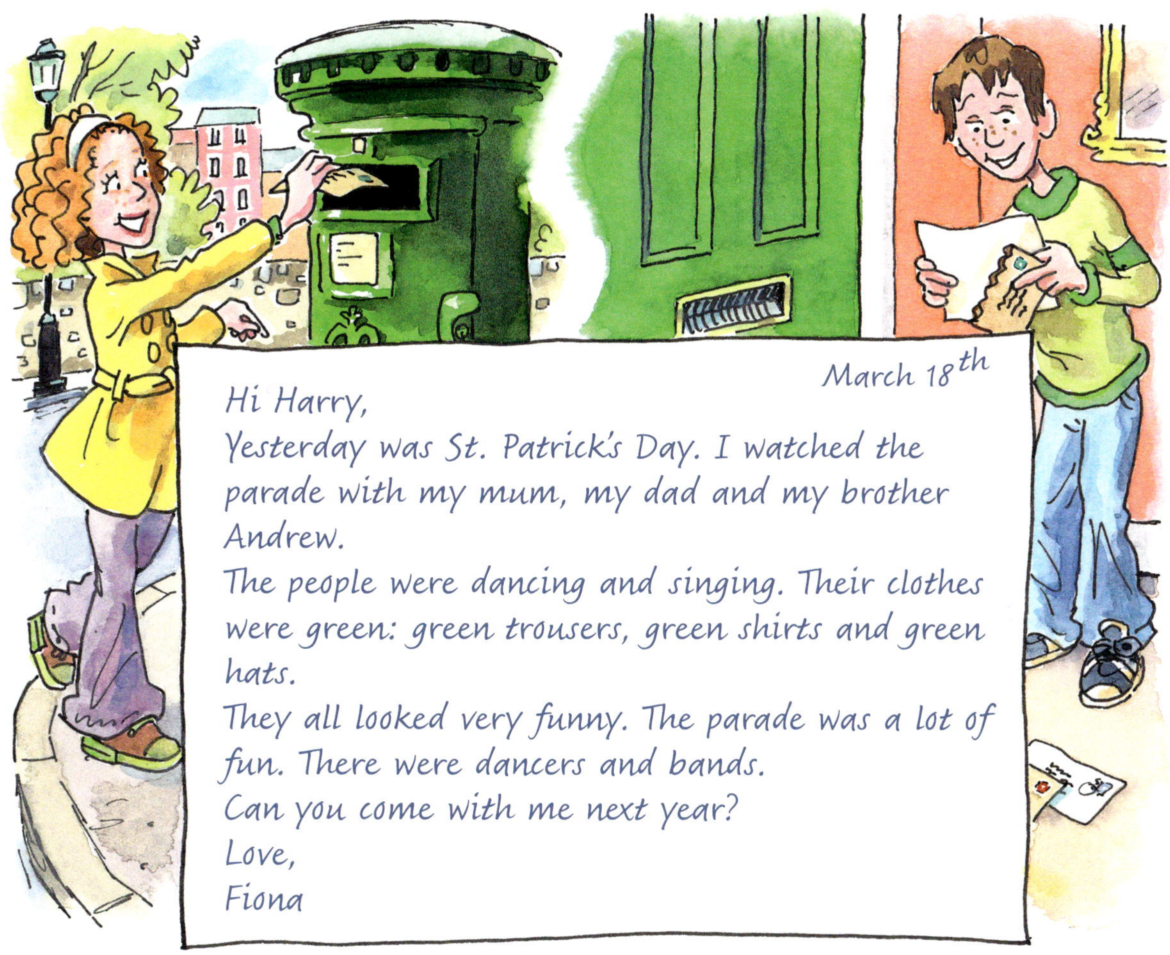

March 18th

Hi Harry,
Yesterday was St. Patrick's Day. I watched the parade with my mum, my dad and my brother Andrew.
The people were dancing and singing. Their clothes were green: green trousers, green shirts and green hats.
They all looked very funny. The parade was a lot of fun. There were dancers and bands.
Can you come with me next year?
Love,
Fiona

Word list

A

a lot of viel, viele
always immer
animal Tier
angry verärgert
autumn Herbst

B

back Rücken
bad schlecht
°**beat** 1. Schlag 2. Pulsschlag
because weil
behind hinter
belly Bauch
bend beugen
°**blow** pusten
boat Boot
bonfire Lagerfeuer
°**bottle** Flasche
bus Bus
bush Busch
but aber
buy kaufen

C

°**candle** Kerze
candy cane Zuckerstange
car Auto
°**cardboard** Pappkarton
caretaker Hausmeister
cent Cent
°**cheese** Käse
°**chili sauce** Chilisoße
city Großstadt
class Klasse
clock tower Glockenturm
cloudy wolkig
club Klub
crocodile Krokodil

D

daffodil Osterglocke
dance tanzen
°**dangerous** gefährlich
Dear Liebe/r
dinosaur Dinosaurier
do judo Judo betreiben
dollar Dollar
door Tür
°**dotted line** gestrichelte Linie
downstairs nach unten, unten
dream Traum

E

ear Ohr
elephant Elefant
email E-Mail
e-pal E-Mail-Freund/in
eye Auge

F

°**face** Gesicht
°**famous** berühmt
favourite Lieblings-
fireworks Feuerwerk
foggy nebelig
foot/feet Fuß/Füße
°**forest** Wald
forward vorwärts
Friday Freitag

G

game Spiel
°**German** deutsch
Germany Deutschland
grandmother Großmutter
grass Gras
Great Britain Großbritannien
gunpowder Schwarzpulver

H

hairdresser Friseur/in
head Kopf
°**helpful** hilfreich
hobby Hobby
°**hole** Loch
holidays Ferien
(at) home zu Hause
hop hopsen/springen

I

inspector Inspektor/in

J

jump hüpfen
jungle Dschungel

K

°**king** König
°**kite** Drachen
knee Knie
know kennen/wissen

L

late spät
leaf/leaves Blatt/Blätter
left links
leg Bein
leprechaun irischer Kobold
°**lettuce** Kopfsalat
lion Löwe
live leben/wohnen
long lang
look sehen
Love 1. Liebe 2. Liebe Grüße

M

°**mask** Maske
°**matches** Streichhölzer
mechanic Mechaniker/in
Monday Montag
monkey Affe
move sich bewegen
mistletoe Mistelzweig
museum Museum
must müssen

N

never nie
nickname Spitzname
notes Notizen

O

often oft
open offen

P

parrot Papagei
password Passwort
°**plane** Flugzeug
play basketball Basketball spielen
play football Fußball spielen
play table tennis Tischtennis spielen
plot Verschwörung
police officer Polizist/in
°**pulse** Puls

Q

°**queen** Königin

R

rainbow Regenbogen
rainy regnerisch
reindeer Rentier
ride a horse reiten
right rechts
river Fluss
rose Rose

S

Saturday Samstag
°**savannah** Savanne
scared verängstigt
sea Meer
second Sekunde
seed Samen/Keim
shamrock Kleeblatt
shop assistant Verkäufer/in
shoulder Schulter
show zeigen
ski Ski fahren
skyscraper Wolkenkratzer
snowdrop Schneeglöckchen
snowman Schneemann
snowy verschneit
°**sour cream** saure Sahne
speak sprechen
spring Frühling
°**staple** klammern
°**stapler** Tacker
°**star** 1. Stern 2. Star
street Straße
stretch dehnen/strecken
°**string** Faden/Schnur
strip Streifen
strong stark
summer Sommer
Sunday Sonntag
sunny sonnig
swim schwimmen

T

table Tisch
table tennis Tischtennis
tail Schwanz
taxi Taxi
taxi driver Taxifahrer/in
teacher Lehrer/in
teeth Zähne
ticket Fahrkarte
Thursday Donnerstag
toe Zeh
train Zug
treason Verrat
°**trunk** 1. Baumstamm 2. Rüssel
Tuesday Dienstag
°**tusk** Stoßzahn

U

underground U-Bahn
up oben
upstairs nach oben, oben
USA USA (Vereinigte Staaten von Amerika)
°**useful** nützlich

W

°**wax** Wachs
weather Wetter
Wednesday Mittwoch
whale Wal
wheel Rad
wild wild
windowpane Fensterscheibe
windy windig
winter Winter
°**wrap** 1. Hülle 2. Teigfladen
°**wrist** Handgelenk

°Wörter von den *Spotlight*-Seiten